T0011459

Saving

by Ruth Owen

Consultant: Kari Servais
Middle School Family & Consumer Science Educator

BEARPORT
PUBLISHING

Minneapolis, Minnesota

Credits

Cover and title page, © Andrei Barmashov/iStock; 4, © Andrey Arkusha/Shutterstock; 5, © Kardasov Films/Shutterstock; 7, © CEnTo STOCK/Shutterstock; 9, © fizkes/Shutterstock; 11R, © CEnTo STOCK/Shutterstock; 11B, © Africa Studio/Shutterstock; 12, © shippee/Shutterstock; 13, © New Africa/Shutterstock; 15, © Andrey_Popov/Shutterstock; 17, © Rawpixel.com/Shutterstock; 19, © stockfour/Shutterstock; 21, © photastic/Shutterstock; 23, © Twin Design/Shutterstock; 25, © Andrey_Popov/Shutterstock; 27, © Krakenimages.com/Shutterstock; 28B, © VectorArtist7/Shutterstock.

Bearport Publishing Company Product Development Team

President: Jen Jenson; Director of Product Development: Spencer Brinker; Senior Editor: Allison Juda; Editor: Charly Haley; Associate Editor: Naomi Reich; Senior Designer: Colin O'Dea; Associate Designer: Elena Klinkner; Associate Designer: Kayla Eggert; Product Development Assistant: Anita Stasson

Library of Congress Cataloging-in-Publication Data

Names: Owen, Ruth, 1967– author.
Title: Saving / Ruth Owen.
Description: Silvertip books. | Minneapolis, Minnesota : Bearport
  Publishing Company, [2023] | Series: Personal finance: need to know |
  Includes bibliographical references and index.
Identifiers: LCCN 2022032858 (print) | LCCN 2022032859 (ebook) | ISBN
  9798885094191 (library binding) | ISBN 9798885095419 (paperback) | ISBN
  9798885096560 (ebook)
Subjects: LCSH: Saving and investment–Juvenile literature. | Finance,
  Personal–Juvenile literature.
Classification: LCC HG4553 .O94 2023 (print) | LCC HG4553 (ebook) | DDC
  332.024–dc23/eng/20220708
LC record available at https://lccn.loc.gov/2022032858
LC ebook record available at https://lccn.loc.gov/2022032859

For more information, write to Bearport Publishing, 5357 Penn Avenue South, Minneapolis, MN 55419.

Contents

What Is Saving? 4

Smart Saving 6

Make a Plan 8

Bank It 12

Your Money Makes Money 16

That's Interest-ing! 18

When You Can't Save 22

What the Bank Gets 24

It Feels Good to Save 26

Compound vs. Simple Interest 28

SilverTips for Success 29

Glossary 30

Read More 31

Learn More Online 31

Index 32

About the Author 32

What Is Saving?

You want to buy a new laptop, but it's going to cost $700. How will you afford it? You could try earning money by doing chores at home or for neighbors. Set aside some of the cash from each job, and you will eventually have enough. That's saving!

People often save for expensive things they want. But it's smart to save for emergencies, too. What if your phone breaks? If you've saved some emergency money, you can use it for repairs or to buy a new phone.

Smart Saving

After a person gets paid, they must think about how to use their money. They might pay **bills** and buy fun things. Then, they save whatever's left. But what if there's nothing left? It's better to pay for needs first and then save some money. Any leftover money can be spent on fun.

Many bills need to be paid monthly. These might include payments for electricity, water, and internet. People usually do not save for these needs. They just plan to pay for them every month.

Make a Plan

A plan for money is called a **budget**. It shows **income**, or the money someone makes. The budget also shows how that money will be spent. People use budgets to make sure they're not spending more than they're earning. Budgets help plan for savings, too.

Any time you get money, you have a choice. You could spend it or save it. You may even want to **invest** it. Then, your money might make you more money.

It's important to check a budget regularly to make sure spending and saving stays on track.

People often budget to save for specific things they need or want. The amount of money a person hopes to save is called a savings goal. It may take a long time to save for a large goal, such as the cost of a new car. Savings goals for smaller things take less time.

Many people save for more than one thing at a time. A short-term savings goal could pay for a gift for a friend. A long-term goal might go toward an expensive bike.

Bank It

How do you save money? One way is to put it in a savings **account** at a bank. Most banks will **limit** how often you can take money out of the account. A savings account is a good way to keep yourself from spending the money you're trying to save.

An easy way to reach small savings goals is to put aside spare change. Don't spend it for a while. A few coins here and there will add up.

Sometimes, people set up an **automatic transfer** to a savings account. This means some of their money is moved into their savings on a schedule. For example, money from their paycheck may go into a **checking account** each month. Then, a set amount moves from that checking account into their savings.

Having money in a checking account lets you pay for things easily. Just write a check or swipe a debit card.

Your Money Makes Money

When your money is in a savings account, it will earn **interest**. This is money that the bank pays you! The amount of interest is a small percent of what's in the savings account. That percent is called the interest rate.

Why do banks pay interest? It's because they use people's savings. Banks **lend** the money to other people. In return for using money from savings accounts, banks pay these people a little extra.

That's Interest-ing!

Savings accounts have two types of interest. The first is called simple interest. It is paid only on the amount that someone puts into their account. For example, a savings account might earn 5 percent simple interest per year. This means an account that starts with $1,000 will earn $50 interest a year.

If a person leaves their savings in the bank, the money will keep earning interest. In two years, savings of $1,000 at 5 percent simple interest will earn $50 twice. The savings grows to $1,100.

Different banks may offer different interest rates for savings accounts.

The second type of interest is called compound interest. This is paid on the total amount in an account. It includes money you put into your account as well as the amount earned from previous interest payments. Someone who has saved $1,000 plus $50 of interest will then be paid interest on $1,050.

Compound interest can build up savings faster. At 5 percent simple interest, $1,000 would grow to $1,250 over 5 years. But at 5 percent compound interest, $1,000 would become $1,276 in 5 years.

$368.74

$520.3

$258.96

$1,585.07

$305.01

$513.55

$1,567.48

$925.32

$137.95

$424.72

$204.56

$1,069.07

$112.90

$11,051

Many savings accounts earn a
little bit of interest every month.

When You Can't Save

Saving takes time. If you need to buy something right away, you could borrow money. However, when you borrow from banks, you have to pay *them* interest. This means you'll end up paying more than the amount you originally borrowed.

Sometimes, people have to borrow money because they don't have time to save for something they need right away. This may happen during an emergency.

What the Bank Gets

The interest rate someone pays for borrowing is usually higher than the rate earned on a savings account. Why? It's a way for banks to make money. A bank may charge borrowers 10 percent interest. At the same time, it could pay only 5 percent to people's savings accounts. Then, the bank keeps the rest.

Credit cards are a common way to borrow money. When a shopper uses a credit card, their purchases are paid for by the bank. Then, the shopper pays the bank back. They may have to pay interest.

It Feels Good to Save

Saving isn't always easy. If you keep money in savings, you may have less to spend on fun. Waiting for things you want can feel difficult, too. However, planning and saving will make you better at managing your money. And hitting your savings goals feels great.

Want to try an easy way to save? Some apps do a lot of the work for you. An app might round up all your payments and put the extra money into a savings account.

Compound vs. Simple Interest

A savings account can help you make the most of your money. But do you want simple interest or compound interest? Let's take a look at how $100 grows with each type of interest at a rate of 5 percent.

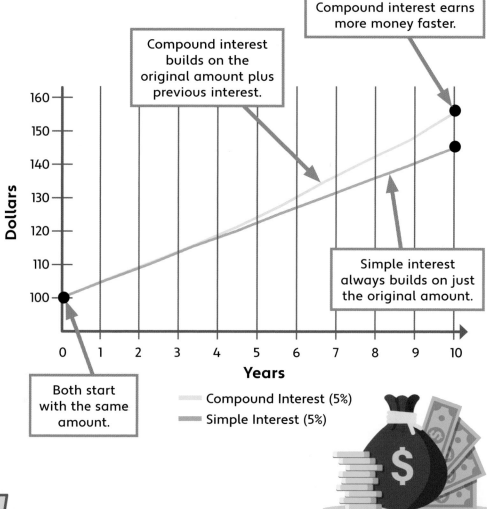

Compound interest earns more money faster.

Compound interest builds on the original amount plus previous interest.

Simple interest always builds on just the original amount.

Both start with the same amount.

Dollars

160 —
150 —
140 —
130 —
120 —
110 —
100 —

0 1 2 3 4 5 6 7 8 9 10

Years

Compound Interest (5%)
Simple Interest (5%)

★ SilverTips for REVIEW

Review what you've learned. Use the text to help you.

Define key terms

borrow

checking account

compound interest

savings account

simple interest

Check for understanding

What is a savings goal, and how might goals differ?

What is the difference between simple interest and compound interest?

Describe two ways to save money.

Think deeper

Make a budget, including plans to set aside money for a savings goal. Given your budget, how long will it take to reach your goal?

★ SilverTips on TEST-TAKING

- **Make a study plan.** Ask your teacher what the test is going to cover. Then, set aside time to study a little bit every day.

- **Read all the questions carefully.** Be sure you know what is being asked.

- **Skip any questions** you don't know how to answer right away. Mark them and come back later if you have time.

Glossary

account an arrangement in which a bank holds money and keeps track of it

automatic transfer the scheduled movement of money from one account to another

bills documents that show how much is owed for a service

budget a plan for your money that includes income and spending

checking account a kind of bank account where money can be added and taken out regularly

income money a person makes from a job

interest extra money that is paid to borrow or use someone else's money

invest to spend money on something with the goal of getting more money back

lend to give someone money that they must pay back

limit to keep something from going beyond a set amount

Read More

Cavell-Clarke, Steffi. *Spending and Saving Money (Our Values).* New York: Crabtree Publishing, 2019.

London, Martha. *Saving and Investing (Money Basics).* San Diego, CA: BrightPoint Press, 2020.

Reina, Mary. *Save Money (Earn It, Save It, Spend It!).* North Mankato, MN: Pebble, 2020.

Learn More Online

1. Go to **www.factsurfer.com** or scan the QR code below.

2. Enter "**Saving**" into the search box.

3. Click on the cover of this book to see a list of websites.

Index

bills 6

borrowing 22, 24

budgets 8–10

checking accounts 14

credit cards 24

emergencies 4, 22

goals 10, 12, 26

income 8

interest 16, 18–22, 24, 28

needs 6, 10, 22

savings accounts 12, 14, 16, 18–21, 24, 26, 28

wants 4, 8, 10, 26

About the Author

Ruth Owen has written hundreds of nonfiction books. She lives on the Cornish coast in England with her husband and three cats.